GREAT MASTERS OF FANTASY ART

TACO

Printed and bound in Berlin
ISBN: 3-89268-008-6
Cover Illustration: Boris Vallejo: The Flying Serpent
Backcover Illustration: Paul Lehr: Untitled

£18

GREAT MASTERS OF FANTASY ART

TEXT BY
ECKART SACKMANN

TACO

CONTENTS

INTRODUCTION

Man has always been very proud of his intellect as something that sets him apart from other creatures on this planet. But time and again he has also tried to break free from the restraints which are imposed on him by his intellect. It would be a rather poor world if it were fully comprehensible to us in all its aspects. Such a world would be tedious and insipid, not only for homo sapiens with his inexhaustible thirst for knowledge, but also for homo ludens with his aesthetic sense and his creativity.

Man is a dreamer. He has need for the irrational, and if his humdrum everyday life does not allow him to satisfy this need, then he is in fact quite capable of drawing on his own imagination. If he has a particular artistic talent, he wants to pass his dreams on to other people, be it in the form of literature or of pictures. Indeed, there is so much variety that there can be no doubt about the immeasurable wealth and power of man's imagination.

The rationalist tendency of our world has been counterbalanced by fantasy literature ever since man first learned to communicate by means of a writing system. Take, for instance, the Babylonian Gilgamesh Epic of the third millenium B.C.: from our modern point of view it is extremely imaginative and full of fantasy elements.

But when we use the word fantasy, we really mean a far more recent development. It is a genre which came into being in the 1960s as an off-shoot of science fiction.

Science fiction was undergoing considerable changes at the time. Space travel had given mankind a number of real experiences, and more and more people had come to the conclusion that "progress" was somewhat dubious both in this area and in other spheres of technology. As a result, science fiction authors began to focus more on the "software" of mankind than on the "hardware" it could produce. If a writer was ambitious, he would no longer concentrate on the bold conquest of the infinite universe, i.e. of outer space, but rather on the "inner" space of human activities and thought patterns.

This development meant that science fiction literature could no longer be pigeon-holed as pulp literature by literary critics of a more traditional persuasion. It was no longer possible to draw a clear and rigid dividing line between light and serious literature. J.R.R. Tolkien, for example, who achieved an incredible degree of popularitay with his fantasy epic **The Lord of the Rings,** is one such case, because we cannot really classify him in terms of the one category or the other.

Nevertheless we can make a basic distinction between two major streams of recent fantasy literature. The one has been called **sword and sorcery fantasy** or **heroic fantasy** (a later term). They are mainly about tough adventures which take place in an imaginary barbarian world where technology and civilization are at their lowest level. The other type has been called **high fantasy,** with a generally higher degree of literary quality. This is where we can place Tolkien.

There is, however, one common denominator in all fantasy literature: it is always set in a different world, i.e. in an imaginary sphere that does not follow the same rational principles as our own. Most of it is about a quest for adventure, and it upholds certain values of different kinds, with themes that draw on traditional legends that also included elements of fantasy.

This imaginary world has been expressed visually by fantasy art. Its original function was to illustrate literature, and what we said about fantasy literature is therefore also true for pictures. The older generation of fantasy artists, such as Frank Kelly Freas and Paul Lehr, all started off as illustrators of science fiction books.

But even the younger artists introduced in this collection were in many respects influenced by science fiction. Quite a few of today's illustrators grew up in the fifties, when people were continuously striving for more and more knowledge, when the two superpowers were fighting for supremacy in outer space, and when these two topics were the ones that most impressed and preoccupied everyone, particularly the mass media.

As in other spheres of art, it soon became clear in fantasy art who was going to survive beyond the first moments of initial enthusiasm and be influential in years to come. This collection of illustrations is to give some idea of the different styles that exist within a genre that has by now assumed international proportions. You will see that there is considerable diversity even among these top quality artists who all have their own approaches.

Most illustrations were made as commissions, thus serving different purposes. But added to this, and to the artists' different national and geographical characteristics, it is above all the temperament of the individual that has found its expressions in each picture. When asked where they got their fantastic ideas from, all artists would undoubtedly reply, "My art is part of myself".

As stated above, there is a demand for dreams in our time, which is a reflection of a deficit in our rationalist world. Tolkien once defined fantasy as "overcoming one's poverty of imagination". Fantasy turns towards a different level of consciousness, a level that tends to be suppressed by the perfectionism of "progress" in our everyday life. Thus, it is not so much a matter of looking back but of changing one's viewpoint altogether. With their creative ability to give substance to their dreams, these fantasy artists have succeeded in opening up to us and sharing with us the richness of the worlds they have created.

Fantasy art gives us a glimpse of infinity. Neither forms nor colours are subject to the kind of reality that surrounds us: everything is possible, and everything is true. Time and space become blurred. Whole landscapes are spread out before our eyes, landscapes whose savage beauty and alien sombreness bear witness to the infinite expanses within the human soul. And no two pictures are the same.

The variety of subjects is matched by the diversity of the techniques which the artists employ to capture their fantastic visions. But when we look at these techniques we must always remember that the illustrations are not usually accessible to the onlooker in the form of originals. What the artist actually produces is a master copy which is then printed thousands or millions of times.

Although reprographic methods have to meet certain

standards of excellence, the finished picture can never look exactly like the original. It is rarely the case that the printed picture displays the same shades of colour and the same richness of detail as the master copy. And for the front page of a book it is necessary to reduce the size of the picture considerably. But the amazing thing is that the masters of fantasy art in this book did not in fact take this limiting factor into account right from the beginning. They did not simplify their pictures when they painted them, so that each picture, which is normally only ever seen on the front page of a paperpack, could easily be enlarged to the size of a poster and still maintain the same standards of excellence. So although these illustrations were originally meant for mass production, they are anything but mass products.

Even collectors and art galleries have come to this conclusion by now, and that is why the originals of these pictures – if they are at all available – are so much in demand. Many of these originals are real full-scale paintings, and it is quite obvious that the artists had to go through a fair amount of training, either at a college or by teaching themselves, before they could achieve such expertise and perfection.

Oil is of course used, but many illustrators nowadays also use acrylic, which dries more quickly. Water-colour is very popular, too. But the brush has ceased to be the one and only implement for applying paint, and more and more artists are using the spray gun (airbrush technique), to achieve more subtle shades. It is probably true, to say that most of them use both the traditional brush and the spray gun, and in the hands of an experienced painter a brush can never be an inferior tool.

Boris Vallejo's method of working serves as a good example of how much study and thought are necessary before a picture reaches its final version and presents itself to the eye of the observer in a convincing way. The actual process of painting the picture is very often only the final stage in a lengthy process.

Vallejo usually starts with small pencil sketches which he keeps changing several times until he feels happy with the general composition of the picture. "Sometimes I haven't got any idea of what I'm going to show, but only a feeling of how I want to arrange the elements of a picture and how I want to divide it up." Nobody but the artist himself would ever be able to tell from these sketches what the final picture would eventually be like.

As soon as Vallejo has finished his draft, he starts working with his models. He photographs them in the same poses that he wants the figures in his pictures to have. Originally he used to work with professional models, but now he prefers to ask friends and relations to pose for him. And Vallejo himself can be recognized in many of his illustrations. He then uses these photographs in a very creative way, rather than copying them slavishly.

When he paints the actual picture itself, Vallejo prefers the artificial lighting of neon lights. For the first layer he uses acrylic paint, but he always finishes it off with oil.

Boris Vallejo allows himself between three and six days for each picture. Considering how painstakingly accurate they are, then this seems very little, and yet it is a lot more time than, say, Frank Frazetta takes for his pictures. This shows how different fantasy artists can be, not only in their temperaments but also the techniques they employ.

Illustrators of international repute no longer need to accept just any commission that is offered to them. It used to be the case that the artist had to illustrate whichever book was put in front of him, whereas nowadays it happens quite frequently that a publisher has to find a text which will match the illustrations on his desk.

This is, of course, only true for the stars among the artists. The illustrators on the following pages are such stars of fantasy art. They were the ones whose extraordinary visions have had a profound influence on the designing of modern book covers.

It is in beautiful collections such as this that they are freed from the fetters of commercial art. Fantasy art is an expression of our time, but the masterpieces of this art form will outlive all time.

FRANK FRAZETTA

Frank Frazetta started illustrating book covers because, he says, he was "fed up with all that pencil and ink stuff". But he had spent nearly 20 years with "that pencil and ink stuff", working for different publishing houses of the comics industry. And although his job finally secured him the recognition and praise of art critics, it brought him neither fame nor financial security during the fifties and sixties, in spite of being a top quality artist.

From the early days of his childhood he was considered a real prodigy. Drawing and painting were skills that came to him with remarkable ease. Born of Italian descent in Brooklyn in 1928, this American had absolutely no doubt about the way in which he would earn a living.

Frazetta's true vocation in life, however, did not become apparent until he began his career as an illustrator in 1964. At that time Ace Books were looking for someone to illustrate their latest edition of the Edgar Rice Burroughs Library. And Frank Frazetta was just the right man.

It took this amazing man no more than ten days to design the first six book covers – not because he had been given such a tight deadline, but because he preferred to spend his time playing golf and baseball rather than working! The success of his front covers was so overwhelming that the various publishing companies almost fought for this newly discovered genius. For **Back to the Stone Age Fazetta received the** New York Society of Illustrators **Award of Excellence**.

The artist was now in a position where he could be more selective in his choice of commissions. He made it a matter of principle only to accept a commission if he was given a lot of freedom in his work and if he felt like doing it. After the ERB books, Frazetta designed covers for a variety of books, such as the new horror comics of Warren Publishers and Conan Paperbacks – a subject for which Frazetta was virtually predestined.

To secure a wider circulation of his pictures, Frazetta began to make posters from his oil paintings. But he rigorously refused to part with the originals so that his fans had to make do with reproductions.

Despite the fact that most of his fantasy paintings are considerably reduced in size, one can still sense in them the strength and vitality with which Frazetta tackles the most difficult

Frank Frazetta:
The Galleon

Illustration p. 10-11
Frank Frazetta:
Thuvia, Maid of Mars

© 1975

©74 FRAZETTA

tasks. Apart from his highly effect use of colour, it is above all the dynamism of the movement that immediately enchants the observer.

Frazetta's pictures are practically never static. That is why the majority of them are about subjects which emphasize the savage fierceness of his style, e.g. fighting scenes. And it often seems as if his nightmare-like creatures with their glowing eyes or his fiercely determined barbarian warriors are trying to jump right out of the painting.

Frazetta's art does not just exude a certain atmosphere, it screams at you. It is as if the artist himself was talking directly, as if there was something in his pictures that was also part of the artist. Most of these ingenious illustrations were virtually made at one stroke, some of them within a matter of hours. "I'm working, and the kids are romping about, the dog and the cats keep coming in. It's the noisiest place in the world. But this is how I grew up. I love working with noise. The louder it gets, the faster I work."

Recently Frazetta also tried his hand – successfully – at a cartoon film called **Fire and Ice** by Ralph Bakshi. He is indeed the great magician among fantasy artists. "I want to do something that nobody has done before me. And I want to do it in such a way that nobody will forget me for it..."

Frank Frazetta:
A Princess of Mars

FRAZETTA

FRANK KELLY FREAS

Although Frank Kelly Freas is by far the oldest artist in this anthology, and although he can look back on thirty years of experience as an illustrator, he has nevertheless successfully managed to keep his work up-to-date. Especially the later works of this creator of innumerable science fiction and fantasy illustrations do not differ greatly from those of his younger colleagues. It is worth noting that Tim White, for example, had not even been born when Frank Kelly Freas had already established himself very firmly as an illustrator of book covers.

Frank Kelly Freas, an American, was 28 years old when he produced his first cover in November 1950: it was for the science fiction magazine **Weird Tales.** Shortly afterwards there was hardly any publication of renown within this genre that was not published at least once with a front page designed by Frank Kelly Freas, that incredibly imaginative and resourceful artist. Especially the magazines **Astounding** and **Analog** regularly bore his illustrations on their front pages, and it is undoubtedly true that he helped to make them what they are.

„I really feel like an illustrator rather than a painter,“ Kelly Freas once said about his pictures. "I believe that my pictures and the tales they illustrate should form a unit. Illustrations and text must complement one another. On the other hand I'm not really interested in painting a picture just for the sake of painting it. In the same way that I prefer stories that give me visual impression when I read them, I want my illustrations to tell the onlooker a story.“

Kelly Freas, who was born in New York, tried his hand at a number of completely different jobs, such as engineering and medicine before turning to art. But his artistic talents also turned out to be quite diverse: among other things, he concentrated on photography, television commercials, he painted religious pictures for the order of St. Francis, and pictures for Alfred E. Neumann in **Mad** – and again and again science fiction and fantasy.

One of his most spectacular commissions was that of designing the badge for the first NASA Skylab and a number of posters to popularize American space projects.

It would of course be unthinkable to imagine an artist of his stature without official recognition. Frank Kelly Freas is a kind of regular customer when, year after year, the World Science Fiction Association award their Hugo. So far he has received this award ten times – more often than any other artist before him!

Frank Kelly Freas:
Heretic in a Balloon

KELLY FREAS ©77

GREG HILDEBRANDT

It is not so unusual for twins to be similar in character and temperament. But it probably happens a lot more rarely that they should also have a similar and at the same time extraordinary artistic talent.

Yet this is the sort of talent which the two Americans Greg and Tim Hildebrandt – also known as „The Hildebrandt Brothers“ – have in common. Ever since they made their Tolkien illustrations, if not before, they have been able to attract a large number of fans and fantasy enthusiasts.

The two brothers were born in Detroit in 1939. Early on they developed an interest for the mysterious and the fantastic. "Ever since I can remember, I have always been somehow involved in art," says Greg Hildebrandt. "It began with drawings. Later I tried my hand as a film director. Together with my brother I turned an old barn into a studio where we reconstructed the giant krakens from the Walt Disney film **20.000 Miles under the Sea.** The scene we designed was like that of a world on a strange planet – with craters of vulcanos, mountains and a bright sun in front of a sombre sky. Then we blew it all up."

After Greg had left school, he took an interest in films and film settings for a while. Then he took up a job as a graphic designer in advertising, which still left him enough time to paint pictures and illustrations, together with his brother. These works attracted people's attention and became quite popular, and so in 1978 the two brothers were awarded the gold medal of the Society of Illustrators.

At about the same time Greg and Tim Hildebrandt began to work on a project that was to make them popular far beyond the borders of their own country: the illustration of several calendars with subjects from the fantasy novels by J.R.R. Tolkien. These calendars, of which millions of copies were sold, inspired the Hildebrandts to create their own fantasy novel, **Urshurak,** which of course they illustrated themselves. They invested more than two years in this enormous endeavour.

Besides Urshurak, the two brothers also made other illustrations with the same themes, until in 1981 they decided to part company and develop their art separately.

Greg Hildebrandt remained true to the genre of fantasy. Besides designing the scene of a

Greg Hildebrandt:
Black Cauldron

Illustration p. 20-21
Greg Hildebrandt:
Loki

GREG HILDEBRANDT

fantasy film by Peter Yates, he continued to illustrate book covers. But he also made paintings according to the individual wishes of the people who commissioned them. Such art collectors were not just interested in the clever technique with which Hildebrandt always amazes the onlooker, but also in his choice of subjects, which is so characteristic of this painter.

There are some basic differences between Greg Hildebrandt's fantasy art and that of his colleagues Frazetta and Vallejo with their illustrations in the style of **heroic fantasy.** He is not interested in strong warriors or seductive beauties. His world is a more intimate one, a world of magicians, dwarfs and unicorns against the background of legendary, magic kingdoms. There can be no doubt about Tolkien's influence on his themes.

Greg Hildebrandt is probably the most obvious and outspoken representative of this particular type of fantasy illustration. There is a certain charm in his characteristic distribution of light and shadow and also in his balanced composition, a charm which seems to embody a whole school of painting. In spite of all obvious examples, he has maintained complete autonomy and has even created a style of his own.

Greg Hildebrandt: Rendezvous

GREG HILDEBRANDT

CARL LUNDGREN

"Whenever I paint a picture I want it to challenge the onlooker, I want it to have an effect on him. Only a picture that makes you think will also be successful."

When Carl Lundgren talks about success, he knows what he is talking about. It was without difficulty and within a matter of years that this artist managed to advance to the highest ranks of American fantasy illustrators. The highest point in his career so far came when he was awarded the **Hugo** in 1982, a much sought-after prize for the "best science fiction author of the year".

Lundgren's works can now be seen in galleries and museums, not only in the U.S.A., but also in Europe. Art collectors think of it as a great privilege if they manage to obtain one of the originals of his fantasy illustrations for their collections. Carl Lundgren's single-mindedness in pursuing his ambitions has certainly paid off.

He was born in Detroit in 1947. When he now admits that he had never touched a paint-brush before the age of 17, we find it very hard to believe. The beginning of Carl Lundgren's development, however, proceeded very much along the same lines as that of other young people who are interested in being creative: he played music in clubs, tried his hand as a film director, tried this and tried that.

It did not become obvious to him until after he had left school that he wanted to be an illustrator. After a brief course at the Hollywood Art Center and a correspondence course with the **Famous Artists** he realized that if he wanted to achieve his aims and fulfil his ambition, he would be mainly left to his own resources. But Lundgren did not allow himself to be put off by that.

The late sixties were a time of unrest, and especially in the world of art. Side by side with the established artists, a counter-movement had emerged which consisted largely of young people who were looking for new ways of artistic expression. Lundgren, too, began to design comics and posters for the "alternative" press. He had been living in California and the Midwest, until one day he changed his mind and decided to put together a portfolio of his works and to make himself known to the major publishing houses in New York.

The first few years in New York were rather tough. But suddenly people began to take notice of this man from Detroit. By now he had turned almost completely to the genre he had always liked best: fantasy art. Lundgren's skill in using a variety of techniques now allow him to depict a wide range of fantasy subjects.

"Fantasy art calls for extreme realism", he says about his pictures. "The more realistic a picture, the better – no matter how fantastic the subject may be." This means that Carl Lundgren is about to advance into the ranks of his great examples, illustrators such as Norman Rockwell and Frank Frazetta.

Carl Lundgren:
The Unpleasant Profession of Jonathan Hoag

PANAM

Carl Lundgren:
Master of the Hashomi

CARL
LUND
GREN
1977

Carl Lundgren:
The Nearest Fire

©
CARL
LUND
GREN
1982

OLIVIERO BERNI

For a long time European fantasy illustrators used to be very insignificant compared with their American counterparts. This was probably not because there was less talent on this side of the Atlantic than in America, but rather because American publishing companies had been producing a lot more science fiction and fantasy literature. And illustrations obviously followed this trend. It was only within the last ten years that European artists have managed to catch up with their American colleagues.

Oliviero Berni, born in Milan in 1935, is one of the most important Italian fantasy artists. Having studied at the **Accademia di Brera** and the **Scuola d'Arte del Castello Sforzesco,** Berni became art director of one of Italy's most renowned publishing houses in 1958.

As well as his commissioned work, Berni also painted a large number of abstract pictures in the next few years. These paintings were shown in many art exhibitions both in Italy and abroad. From 1969 Berni turned more and more to the art of illustrating books. It was not long before he discovered where his strengths and weaknesses lay. He soon became internationally famous as a designer of science fiction covers, and so it did not come as a surprise when, in 1980, he was awarded a prize at the Fifth European Science Fiction Congress for the best complete works.

But his prospects were relatively modest compared with the opportunities that were offered to American illustrators. Berni was well aware of this, and as his illustrations had become popular in the States, he decided to move to New York in 1982, where he spent two years working for the best-known publishing companies. And he did not sever these links when, in 1984, he returned to Italy.

Even today he creates most of his fascinating visions for American publishers, and it is only through them that his pictures eventually find their way back to Europe again. With his perfect expertise and ability to handle artistic techniques as well as a diversity of subjects, he certainly ranks as high as American illustrators. He has been able to secure for himself a firm position among the international top of fantasy artists.

Oliviero Berni:
Untitled

BERNI

Oliviero Berni:
Untitled

BORIS VALLEJO

Boris Vallejo started off as the son of a distinguished solicitor in Lima, Peru. Originally he wanted to be a concert violinist, not a painter, and so he took violin lessons for seven years. But then he decided to study medicine and put his violin back into its case. After two years, however, he changed his mind again and applied to the **Escuela Nacional de Bellas Artes,** an art college, where he received a five-year scholarship. It did not take him long to win a much sought after gold medal for his excellent works.

"Drawing has never really been a problem for me. I can't remember a time in my life when I did not actually paint or draw. Art has always been part of myself, a natural expression of my personality."

Vallejo quickly gained in confidence as an artist, and in 1964 he put together a portfolio with some of his works and emigrated to the States – with no more than a few dollars in his wallet. He was hoping for a more awarding career than he could ever have had in Lima. His first job was as an illustrator in the advertising department of a chain store, where he also met Doris, his future wife. After a while, however, he decided to go freelance.

Having designed the title pages for Warren and Marvel's new comic magazines, he then began to work on book covers for several paperback publishing companies. "I had already been working successfully as an illustrator for a few years, when I discovered fantasy art. And suddenly I knew that this was what I wanted to do. I have always had a special love for the perfect structure of the human body, and fantasy art enabled me to depict muscular and sensuous bodies in all variations in my works. And as I love human bodies, I always try to paint them as beautiful and as perfect as possible."

Nearly all his pictures show scenes of savage and effective sensuality. However, it is not just his choice of subjects that soon made him one of the most popular illustrators of his time, but also his perfect expertise as a painter. Since the end of the seventies alone he has designed more than 300 covers, including Tarzan, Conan and the comic magazine Heavy Metal.

His vivid pictures all bear the signature "Boris". And Boris is indeed fully aware of the function of his illustrations. "In the bookshops there are always lots of books side by side, and it is often the cover which decides whether a book is bought or not. A successful cover has to attract the potential customer like a magnet."

A master of his art, Boris uses his erotic pictures to play on the secret lustful desires of his public like a virtuoso on his violin. But just as he knows exactly what to aim for in his paintings, he is also equally inventive and imaginative in them. Boris Vallejo's illustrations are never schematic, flat or lifeless. Unlike any other fantasy artist, he keeps finding more and more ways of tantalizing his public. His inventiveness and versatility seem to know no bounds.

In fact he has not left a single domain of fantasy

Boris Vallejo:
Tarnsman of Gor

BORIS

art untouched. Boris is as familiar with the heroic postures of barbarian warriors as with the poetic ambience of a mysteriously romantic landscape or the frightening sight of bizarre creatures from an alien world.

The composition and colours of these impressive works of art bear witness to the fact that they have been influenced by several hundred years of painting. "Vermeer, Rembrandt, Leonardo – during my early years I used to study the works of such masters again and again. The painters I liked best were two Spanish ones, though: Murillo and Velázquez."

But even today Boris shows great interest in the works of his colleagues. His attitude is anything but complacent and he refuses to rest on his laurels. He keeps watching out for fresh inspiration, continually endeavours to go beyond what he has achieved, and tries to become more and more perfect.

Boris Vallejo:
Best of Leigh Brackett

BORIS

Boris Vallejo:
The Duel

BORIS

Boris Vallejo:
The High Couch of Sillistra

BORIS

RICHARD CORBEN

While most of the well-known fantasy artists were interested in designing book covers right from the beginning, Richard Corben found his way into this genre via comics. It is of course partly due to his immense productivity that there is now such a large number of paintings which were designed as book covers. But the other reason is his remarkable success as an illustrator of unusual picture stories. There can be no doubt that Richard Corben is the star among comic designers today.

However, his beginnings – way back in 1968 – were very modest: he started by publishing his first comic strip in a rather insignificant magazine called **Voice of Comicdom,** and he was already 28 years old. At that time it was only in underground comic magazines such as this one that an artist could have pictures printed that were virtually brimming with sex, irony and violence – the kind that Richard Corben enjoyed painting. It was in such magazines that just about any subject could be chosen – subjects which were closed to the "clean" little booklets available at kiosks, because they were subject to the rules and morals of the Comic Code.

"Underground" meant artistic liberation. It was also a phenomenon that attracted quite a number of artists whose ambitions were artistic rather than financial and who were therefore not really interested in comics that had commercial interests behind them.

But of course even this "art by everyone for everyone" soon had its masters, and Richard Corben was one of them. His magnificent masterpieces soon elevated him high above everybody else. The unique way in which he colours his pictures is based on a complicated technique which he has developed himself. It involves the use of crayons and the spray gun, applying these in several layers of different pictures and copying them together in one single picture.

Corben's subjects are unique, too. Whenever he depicts people, then they are usually monstrously exaggerated in their physique und sexual features. The feelings of these creatures hardly ever seem to go anywhere beyond some very basic emotions, such as hatred, love, greed, lust and anxiety, emotions which often erupt in explosive acts of violence.

With his emphasis on sex and violence, Corben resembles Russ Meyer, the master of cheap films, but at the same time he is also showing a totally alien fantasy world, a world which has got out of hand and which he sometimes puts into a "post-nuclear" setting. This world reflects the complexity of nightmares from our innermost soul.

There is an abundance of animals, mutations and alien fairy-tale creatures in Corben's pictures. "I consciously try to imagine these monsters in such a way that they are different from anything I've ever seen before." Corben's dreams are in fact always frightening; the reader of his comics is never made to feel that he can settle down comfortably and indulge in the delights of some easily digestible entertainment.

The magazines in which Corben publishes his comics have achieved world-wide fame, but with increasing popularity he also began to design more and more book covers and title pages, i.e. individual pictures rather than comic strips. Each of these pictures tells its own story and has a certain immediacy and fascination about it which could only ever be created by a master like Richard Corben.

Richard Corben (with Rick Courtney):
Cover for "Heavy Metal"

©1979
R Corben
R Courtney

VINCENTE SEGRELLES

The fantasy pictures of the Spanish painter Vincente Segrelles are dominated by frightening reptiles and the magic of ornate palaces that seem to come straight from the Arabian Nights. Behind the harsh iciness of cold nature, hostile to the complexities of life, we can see the warm, welcoming lights of human dwelling-places, breathtakingly beautiful as if formed by the hands of fairies. The onlooker is held spell-bound by a world of contradictions, full of grace in its architectural perfection as well as the sobre ruggedness of endless rocky mountains.

The creator of these visions is one of the best-known European fantasy artists. He was born in Barcelona in 1936 and grew up in a family that took great interest in art. His uncle José Segrelles was a famous illustrator.

Vincente, who had already discovered his love for art as a little boy, began a career as a graphic designer and then worked for several advertising agencies. Towards the end of the fifties he managed to get his first illustration accepted, and so he decided to turn his back on advertising and devote his life to designing book covers. Segrelles' unusual subjects soon began to attract people's attention.

His international breakthrough came in 1980, when he published **El Mercenario,** a fantasy story in the form of a comic strip, of which there is now a whole series of albums. **El Mercenario** ("The Mercenary") has already been published in seventeen countries and – together with the works of Richard Corben – is generally recognized as one of the most impressive masterpieces of fantasy comic strips.

What is unusual about Segrelles' comics is the fact that the original copies are real paintings. This is also true for his book covers, but it is most unusual for comics. "I paint in oil, because this is the most convenient technique for me," explains the artist. "The originals of my pictures are about one and a half feet high. Having determined the outlines in a pencil sketch, I then make a rough colour sketch in which I fix the shades of colours I want to use. As soon as that's dry, I start working on the details – a step on which I spend a lot of time and which has to be done very carefully. Finally, the picture is glossed over and cut down to the right size."

Unlike many other fantasy illustrators, Segrelles uses mainly the paintbrush and not the spray gun, which gives his pictures an interesting surface structure. When they are reduced to the size of comics, many subtle shades do, of course, disappear.

His brilliance of composition, which is already evident in each individual picture, becomes even more obvious when we look at his comics where each panel is in tune with the adjoining ones. This makes them very different from any other comics.

But even the subjects of Segrelles' pictures are

Vincente Segrelles: Untitled

extraordinary. His visions of a pre-historic fairy-tale world are based on a well-thought-out concept. Segrelles calls it **fantasia logica** ("logical fantasy"). „I have been doing my best to justify this world inhabited by monstrous reptiles, both to myself and to my public," says the artist.

And this is why the original setting of **El Mercenario** is on a secluded plateau, high up in the Himalayas. Because of its isolation, there have been different influences at work from the rest of the earth, thus resulting in a different development. "The pre-historic reptiles withdrew into the higher regions of the mountains, where they developed into flying dinosaurs. Man domesticated them and began to use them like horses. A totally different kind of civilization came into being, but was destroyed again in a big catastrophe so that we know nothing about it today. But perhaps the infamous Yeti is a remnant of this perished world."

Seductive women, courageous knights and legendary rituals are part of life in this imaginary civilization. Again, there are deliberate contrasts: the soft, warm bodies of his heroines are counterbalanced by the steely coldness of mediaeval armour.

But although there is practically no trace of technological progress in Segrelles' pictures, the people in this pre-historic world are nevertheless sovereign masters over the cruel nature which they are forced to live with. A world full of magic and artistic skill unfolds before our eyes: oriental fairy-tales come back to life, coupled with the dreams and fantasies of a contemporary artist. "Heroic fantasy", Segrelles confesses, "is no more than the way in which I can transform my own fantasies into art".

Vincente Segrelles:
From "El Mercenario"

Vincente Segrelles:
Untitled

Vincente Segrelles:
Untitled

BARCLAY SHAW

It only took Barclay Shaw three years to advance to the top ranks of fantasy illustrators in New York. Three times in a row – 1983, 1984 and 1985 – he was awarded the **Hugo,** the prize for the best science fiction artist. He has had commissions from virtually every single publishing house of this genre, not only for books but also for magazines. Barclay Shaw was born in Bronxville, New York, in 1949. After taking his degree in religious philosophy he spent a few years as a sculptor, until he moved to Colorado in 1975. "I worked there as a freelance artist, designer, carpenter, dishwasher – anything I was offered", says Shaw, looking back on this rather turbulent time in his life. Then he returned to the east coast, where he spent a short time as a cabinet maker before enrolling at the well-known School of Art and Design in New England in 1977.

Versatile as he was, he also used to earn some extra money working for an advertising agency, where he soon attracted attention because of his talent and his skilled use of the airbrush technique. When the agency needed someone to design a poster with illustrations for the film **Close Encounters of the Third Kind,** Barclay Shaw was exactly the right man for the job. In the years to come he designed several different title pages for the **Magazine of Fantasy and Science Fiction** and finally came to the conclusion that if he ever wanted to be really successful as an illustrator, he had to move to New York, the centre of the American publishing world.

Shaw never regretted this decision. In New York he was spotted by Harlan Ellison, an internationally famous author, who was so enthusiastic about Shaw's works that he asked his publisher to have the covers of his books designed by Barclay Shaw in the future. The close co-operation between author and illustrator was to the mutual advantage of both. Shaw's style, as shown in eighteen book covers for Harlan Ellison, was a mixture of fantasy and realism and turned out to be a good basis for his career.

The people whom Shaw regards as his examples include contemporary illustrators such as Rowena Morril and Michael Whelan, but also the great masters of previous centuries: Hieronymus Bosch, Leonardo da Vinci and the Pre-Raffaelites.

Barclay Shaw:
Martian Way

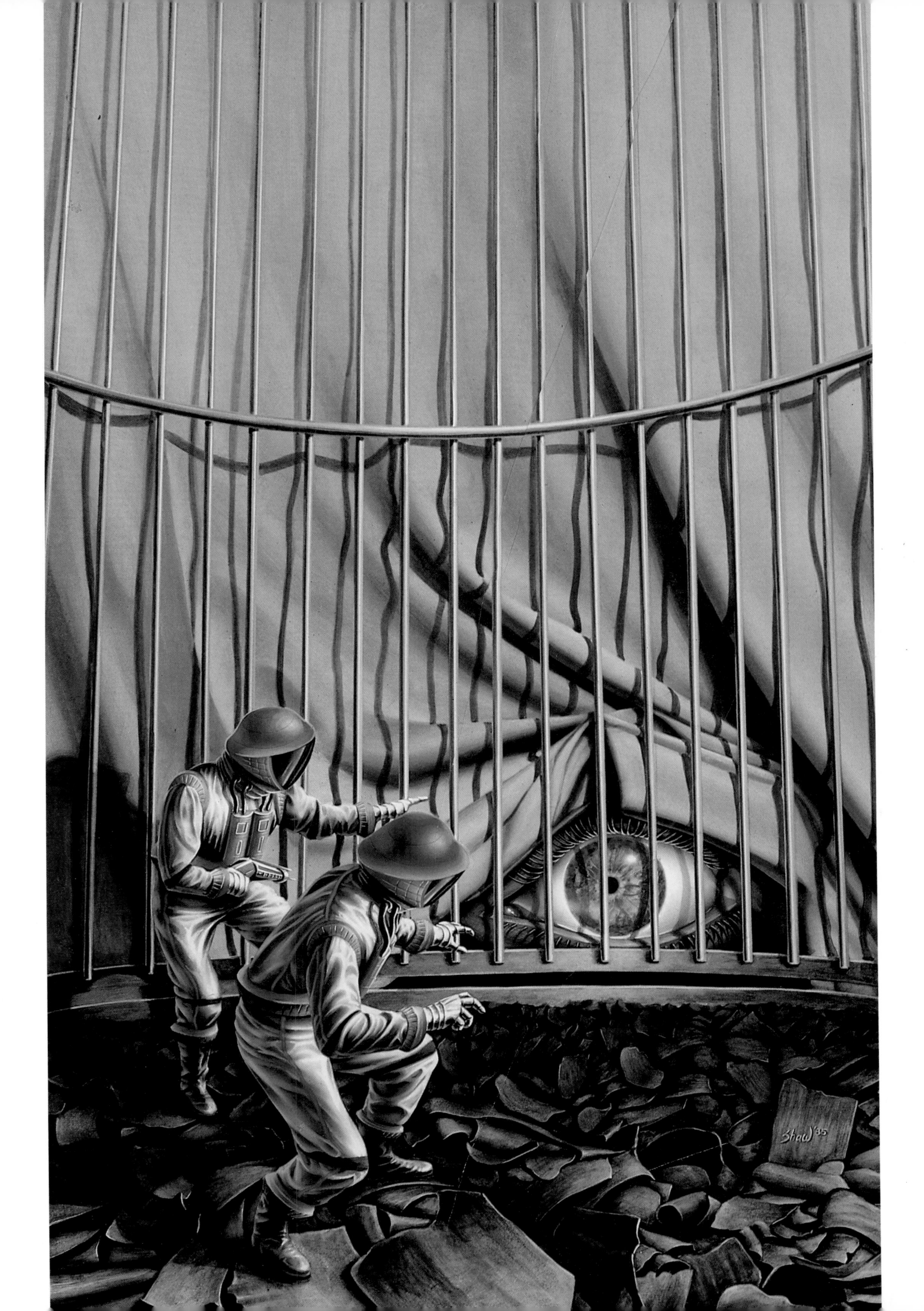
Shaw '85

Barclay Shaw:
Limits

Barclay Shaw:
The Remaking of S. Freud

ROWENA MORRILL

Fantasy illustrators have often been accused of a male bias in their visions, painting mainly muscular heroes who rule over imaginary empires with a cruel and strong hand, surrounded by beautiful girls whose sole function is that of looking pretty and decorative. But ever since Rowena Morrill started to paint, this criticism has been invalid.

Rowena Morrill is 42 years old and an American. Her pictures are of the same quality as those of her male colleagues, and it took her a very short time to advance to the position of a top illustrator among fantasy artists. Some critics soon began to call her „the female Boris Vallejo", but anyone who has ever looked at her art in detail will have to acknowledge her independence and originality. Her paintings cover a wide range of subjects, which can be explained partly by the fact that she has been getting so many commissions from so many publishers that she hardly knows where to start.

There are of course the usual heroic fantasy themes, looking back to a fictitious barbaric age. But at the same time there is also a very large number of fascinating paintings in which Rowena depicts the world of magic, conjuring up occult powers, both benevolent and evil. Her imagination has brought forth some ghastly monsters and worms with sharp claws and long tongues – a nightmare world, which has reached horrifying proportions, seizes people with terror and threatens to devour them.

Other pictures, on the other hand, have something ironical about them, such as the colossal figure on his throne in **Timebender**. The figure is looking down rather contemptuously at the frightened little man with his axe who seems almost like a mouse before a cat. And, in fact, Rowena has not only illustrated all kinds of fantasy subjects, but also a considerable number of science fiction books.

If it comes as a surprise that this artist should be so versatile, then it will probably be no less surprising to learn about her artistic career. Her family consisted almost entirely of musicians, and so she began by studying the piano. However, at the age of 17, she gave up her course and married a soldier.

Being a soldier's wife must have been rather dull at times, and so Rowena readily agreed when

Rowena Morrill:
The Dreaming Jewels

a neighbour invited her to come to a drawing course with her. This course had been organized by the wives' club of the air force base where the Morrills were living at the time. Rowena was 21 and had never held a crayon in her life. Nevertheless, she surprised her teacher by turning out to be extraordinarily talented and drawing as if she had never done anything else in her life.

From this moment art became a vocation for Rowena, a vocation which she followed as if she were obsessed by it. Her pictures became more and more perfect and she managed to meet the most difficult demands. (Incidentally, she is left-handed.) Naturally, fame and prestige soon followed. The name Rowena Morrill became well-known, not only in the States but also abroad.

If, however, Rowena can be trusted in what she says about her own art, then she has been keeping a certain inner aloofness from the dream-like visions she depicts in her paintings. This is why there is a certain remoteness in the bodies of characters she has been creating. No blood seems to flow through the veins of these creatures, their perfect sinews are covered with a skin that is almost metallic, and the emotions reflected in their faces show very little warmth. The onlooker hardly ever feels part of Rowena's monstrous visions, and yet he is somehow affected and frightened by these confusing things that are happening in a completely different world.

Rowena

Rowena Morrill:
Untitled

Rowena

Rowena

RODNEY MATTHEWS

It is often everyday objects that seem extraordinary to us. Looked at closely, an old piece of wood can suddenly seem like a gigantic chain of rugged mountain peaks. With some imagination, a peace of paper can look like the horrifying wing of a primaeval dragon.

Rodney Matthiews' bizarre pictures are full of such everyday objects, exaggerated, re-arranged and changed out of recognition by manipulating their shapes and colours. Thus they are removed from the here and now and become part of Matthews' fantasy world.

„Some people believe that I find the subjects for my pictures in my dreams or even use drugs to inspire me. But that's not true. I can hardly ever remember my dreams, and what I need to work is above all a clear head. Usually I get my inspiration from natural shapes, and I've already collected a whole photographic archive of all the things that have somehow struck me".

With a bit of effort we can often see what it was that must have served Matthews as a starting point for a picture. That does not make his works any less extraordinary or fascinating.

His subjects range from cool science fiction and views of other-worldly landscapes to legends of the Tolkien variety. And yet all these illustrations have one common denominator which bears witness to the idiosyncratic in Rodney Matthews' art.

Matthews, who was born in the south-west of England in 1945, comes from a family which had always taken an active interest in art. The rural environment where he grew up gave him ample opportunity as a child to study nature in all its aspects, and the school subjects that interested him were above all the creative ones.

After his A'levels Matthews decided to go to Bristol Art College. An advertising agency gave this ambitious artist the necessary practice and also his first opportunity to earn a living, but the quality of his work soon enabled him to build up contacts with various publishers who asked him to design book covers and title pages.

He also designed a number of record sleeves, as well as numerous special scripts and signets. It was in his signets that Matthews showed his strength, giving close attention to detail and incorporating legendary creatures and science fiction elements. His works have met with great acclaim, both in Britain and abroad.

Michael Moorcock, the famous science fiction author for whom Matthews has created a whole series of book covers, says: „Looking back on the illustrations which Rodney has designed within the last few years alone, then it's really amazing how many there are and how much of a range there is. I know that these pictures are already very popular with art collectors, but I think the ability and the popularity of this artist will increase even more within the next few years."

Rodney Matthews:
Stop the Slaughter

Illustration p. 68--69
Rodney Matthews:
Drumboogie

Illustration p. 70-71
Rodney Matthews:
Mirador

PAUL LEHR

Like many others of today's fantasy illustrators, Paul Lehr started his career with science fiction „space" pictures. He is American, and when he started his career in 1958, space travel had just aroused fresh interest among the public because of the success of contemporary space projects.

Lehr remembers how he put together the modell for his first cover: "I constructed my 'spaceships' from all kinds of stuff – such as ping pong balls – and then painted this construction like other artists paint still lives. Then I took one of these paintings along to Bantam Books, and it became my first book cover."

Paul Lehr was 28 at the time, and this was the beginning of a permanent and rewarding job as an illustrator. Since then, he says, he has designed about four to five thousand book covers. He can no longer remember the exact number. With increasing routine, there has of course been a change in his methods of putting together pictures. By now he is not so much interested in the stark forms of spaceships, but rather the depiction of a fantasy world which follows different laws of nature from ours.

As an illustrator, however, Lehr frequently has to submit to the ideas of the publisher, who often has a rather precise notion of what a particular book cover should look like, while a different publisher may want to give him as much scope as the text of the book allows.

"In most cases I've got the freedom to give the reins to my imagination and to interprete the story I've been asked to illustrate so that it is in keeping with my feelings about it." A painter thinks above all in pictures, so Lehr aims not so much at a truthful rendering of the text, but rather a depiction of the visual inspiration a subjects gives him.

Paul Lehr, whose visions are more in demand than ever, is a true professional among the science fiction and fantasy illustrators. One of his private hobbies, however, reminds us of the humble beginnings of his career: he enjoys gathering together all kinds of different objects on his farm in Pennsylvania and then putting them together in bizarre constructions, sculptures of an abstract kind. In this way he can give three-dimensional expression to his amazing imagination.

Paul Lehr: Untitled

RICHARD HESCOX

When we look at Richard Hescox's pictures, it is immediately obvious that he has not been following contemporary examples. There is something pleasantly old-fashioned about Hescox's calm, traditional composition and the delicate colour schemes in his paintings.

"I'm not particularly interested in modern art," says Hescox, trying to explain why he deliberately prefers more conventional techniques. "I'd rather go back to eighteenth century painting. I'm a romantic artist for whom academic correctness is a basic principle in art. I do, however, try to create something picturesque, i.e. to give an impression of realism by means of using simple colours."

Hescox was born in Pasadena, California, in 1949 and trained to become an illustrator at the Los Angeles Art Center, where he studied Art, Drawing and Painting. During that time he consciously chose the influences that moulded him among classical American artists, such as Howard Pyle, as well as the academically composed paintings of the late Pre-Raffaelite Waterhouse. At the same time he began to develop a taste for fantasy subjects.

To earn a living, he and his friends Rick Hoppe and William Stout applied for jobs as portrait-painters at Disneyland. The experience they gained here was subsequently put to good use when the three artists began to work on comics and then presented their pictures at the 1973 San Diego Comic Art Convention. It was Hexcox's good fortune that the famous comics illustrator Neal Adams was also at the convention and liked his work very much indeed.

Adams recommended this budding young talent to Marvel, the most dominant comics publisher on the American market. It was a unique opportunity for Hescox when he was asked to illustrate the covers of a number of **Conan** magazines and of **Vampire Tales** – an opportunity which he did not fail to take. It was soon followed by commissions from several paperback publishers, such as a whole series of fantasy covers for DAW Books.

"I like fantasy and science fiction subjects best. The DAW commission allowed me to paint lots of male and female 'barbarians', which I liked very much, of course." Hescox enjoys depicting his female figures as demonic witches, whereas he prefers to show his male heroes as bold conquerors. But there is no one-sided fixation in the choice of his topics on "Sword and Sorcery Fantasy", as is obvious from the illustrations in this book.

Unlike the majority of his colleagues, Hescox preferred not to go to New York, that Mecca of illustrators. He is now living in Los Angeles, where he also works for the film industry.

Richard Hescox:
Untitled

Hescox ©77

Richard Hescox:
Untitled

Richard Hescox:
Untitled

TIM WHITE

British science fiction and fantasy publishers have always had the great advantage of being able to take over American material without having to translate it. But this stimulus soon gave birth to an independent British development, both in the field of literature and illustrations.

For a long time, starting at the beginning of the seventies, British science fiction magazines were dominated by pictures of spacecrafts, as painted by illustrators like Chris Foss. Fascinating though they were, their cool technological touch also had something rather impersonal and sterile about it. It was, however, a style which was imitated by quite a lot of artists.

Few of them were in fact as perfect in their endeavours as Tim White, who was closer to the original example than any of them. But White's standards were too high for him to continue copying somebody else's style for too long. He had always been interested in fantasy, and this is where some of his most beautiful pictures can be found.

Tim White was born in Kent in 1952, and after his A-levels he studied General Illustration at the Medway College of Art. He was not even twenty years old when he managed to sell his first poster. During his time at college, far away from the hectic rush and pressure that is so often part of the life of an illustrator, he could develop his own style and experiment with different subjects and techniques.

In 1972 he joined an advertising agency where he gained a lot of experience which came in useful later on. His skills soon enabled him to go independent, however, and to become a freelance illustrator. Since then he has designed a large number of book covers, record sleeves and film sets.

Tim White has been able to show his fantasy pictures at a number of exhibitions, where they impressed people with their perfect technique and their awesome mystical beauty. Tim White has already acquired a reputation as one of the most outstanding British fantasy artists.

Tim White:
Stranger in a Strange Land

Tim White:
Barbie Murders

MICHAEL WHELAN

Michael Whelan, who was born in Culver City, California, in 1950, is probably the most successful one among the younger generation of American fantasy artists. His father was an aircraft technician, which meant that the family had to keep moving to and fro between California and Colorado. Michael had probably inherited his father's enthusiasm for the progress that was being made in air and space travel, and when he was a little boy, he used to build little wooden "space crafts" to fly to Mars.

After graduating from high school he studied biology and art at San José State University. To finance his course he constructed, among other things, anatomical models for the biology department, but concentrated more and more on art.

In 1974 he took up postgraduate studies at the Art Center College in Los Angeles. After a few months, however, he had convinced his teachers that there was hardly anything they could teach him. So he left the college again and began to look around for an opportunity to make a fortune with his talents.

Michael Whelan did not have to wait for long. It was in the same year that he was asked to design a title page for DAW Books, a New York-based publishing house. This was soon followed by commisions from other publishers as well as exhibitions at art galleries where Whelan could show the magnificent originals of his cover illustrations.

This young, talented artist from California had suddenly become a celebrity. He has received a number of awards for his work, including the two most coveted ones, the **Hugo** for the most prominent science fiction artist as well as the **Howard** for the best fantasy artist.

One of the distinguishing marks of his paintings is his close attention to detail, both with regard to technique and subject-matter. His depiction of space is reminiscent of the famous **Sfumato** elements in Leonardo da Vinci's compositions – an impression which is achieved by the tangible depth and forceful atmosphere which the artist creates on the canvas.

The subjects of his illustrations are often taken from the world of legends and are extremely expressive. His pictures are an excellent compromise between the straightforward adventure stories which he illustrates and the demands of High Fantasy. Michael Whelan's pictures are very popular collectors' items among the connoisseurs of fantasy art.

Michael Whelan:
The Man Who Counts

Michael Whelan:
The Amazing Dragon

DON MAITZ

"To me, being a fantasy artist means escaping from the shackles of realism and freely depicting what goes on inside me. I want to entertain by making unlimited use of all my dreams and fantasies. Of course, when you design a book cover, you have to let yourself be guided by what the author wants to say in his tale. My idea, however, is that when people pick up a book and look at the cover, they get more than an inkling of what the novel is about. I want them to be entertained by my illustration."

Don Maitz was born in Bristol/Connecticut, U.S.A., in 1953. After school he went to the Paier School of Art, where he graduated as the best student of his year in 1975.

"When I first took an interest in art, I asked myself which genre I would enjoy most: portraits, landscapes, still lives or abstract art? Should I paint impressionist, realist or surrealist pictures? I soon learnt that I couldn't really commit myself anywhere and that I'd have to find a field of activity which would give me freedom."

This is how Don Maitz came to be a fantasy illustrator. His talent and unusual power of imagination enabled him to hold his own against his fellow-competitors. Within a very short time he succeeded in making a name for himself as an illustrator of book covers. In 1980 he was awarded the silver medal of the Society of Illustrators and the **Howard**, the prize of the World Fantasy Convention for the best fantasy artist of the year.

Although he has remained true to his original intention not to commit himself to any particular style or subject, his pictures nevertheless reveal the unmistakable hand of a great master. The high standard of his paintings has led to a considerable demand from galleries and museums to exhibit his works. For quite a while now Don Maitz's art has been liked and admired both in the States and outside its borders.

Don Maitz:
Untitled

Maitz

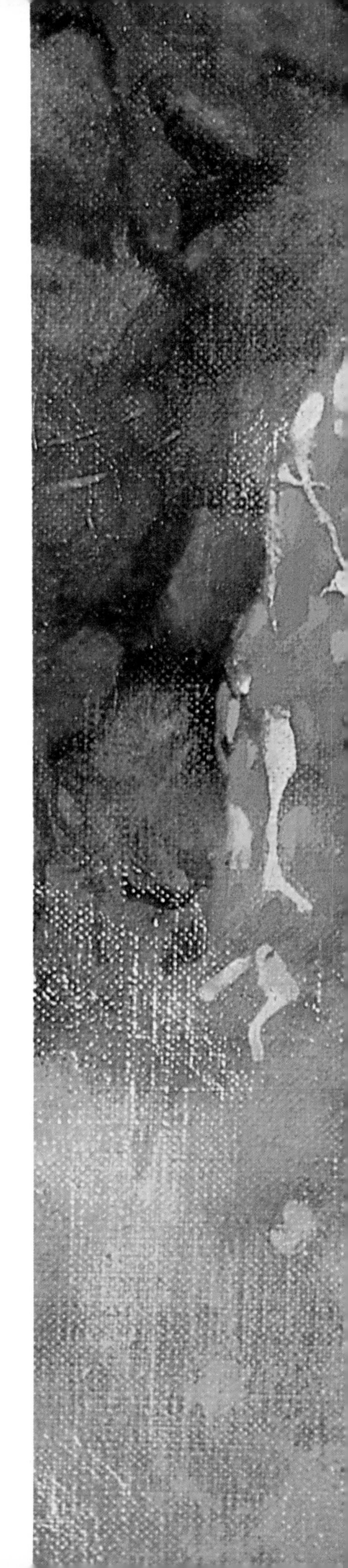

Don Maitz:
Untitled

Don Maitz:
Untitled